C.N. GREGG

DIVORCE MADE SIMPLE

**The Ultimate Guide on How to Survive Divorce,
Learn the Best Approach and Useful Tips on How
to Get Out of Your Divorce in One Piece**

Descrierea CIP a Bibliotecii Naționale a României
C.N. GREGG
    DIVORCE MADE SIMPLE. The Ultimate Guide on How to Survive Divorce, Learn the Best Approach and Useful Tips on How to Get Out of Your Divorce in One Piece / C.N. Gregg – Bucharest: Editura My Ebook, 2021
    ISBN

C.N. GREGG

DIVORCE MADE SIMPLE

The Ultimate Guide on How to Survive Divorce, Learn the Best Approach and Useful Tips on How to Get Out of Your Divorce in One Piece

My Ebook Publishing House
Bucharest, 2021

CONTENTS

NO-ONE REALLY WANTS DIVORCE

You didn't walk down the aisle with the intention of being divorced. You chose your mate because you thought it was with the understanding of being together all your lives. However sometimes things just don't work out and the only way to be free of an unhappy relationship or marriage is the final act of divorce.

Marriage and Divorce Statistics

In the United States these are the latest figures regarding marriage and divorce according to the US Census Bureau dated 2009.

> **Marriage Rate** = 6.8 per 1,000 for the total population. Number of **Marriages:** 2,096,000. **Divorce Rate** = 3.6 per 1,000 populations (There were 44 reporting States and Washington D.C.) From these figures it seems for every marriage there was also half the amount of divorces. Those are some pretty high statistics.

Domestic Abuse

Statistics say that one in four women will experience domestic violence at some point in their lives. One in 3 women will fall victim to a homicide by a spouse or partner through domestic violence. Men in same sex relationships will also be at higher risks of experiencing abuse. Approximately 3 million children will witness domestic violence in their home every year in the USA.

The figures above are not only frightening but an ugly realty of what actually can happen in divorce. Staying alert with an ex-partner, husband or wife can be one of the smartest moves to make. We are not saying to become fearful but rather be on alert for certain patterns in behavior, fits of anger, depression and other factors that can trigger huge changes through divorce.

People can change dramatically when going through the divorce process and the person we always thought we knew, can turn into someone dark and sometimes sinister.

Of course there are other factors that make divorce even more stressful like lawyers, counselors, custody of the children and the split of finances. Of course people will more than likely change with the ups and downs like this, which is something most of us expect. Most of us are never ready for the worse side of people to come out through a divorce either.

We hope this guide can be a source for good materials related to awareness and defense if need be. We hope help you through the rocky road of divorce and arm yourself with those Guerilla Warfare Tactics that may arise to help in the defense of yourself, children and your home.

"If there is an underlying relationship between domestic violence and divorce regime, we would expect to observe changing violence propensities in the treatment group relative to the controls. Because the survey universe consists only of couples living in a conjugal unit, we are limited to analyzing rates of domestic violence within intact marriages. Crime victimization survey data both lack state identifiers and are not available for the relevant time period. Police reports suffer both from serious problems of under-reporting and, more importantly, changes in social norms regarding reporting over the relevant time period." Murray A. Straus and Richard J. Gelles, quote from **"Physical Violence in American Families"**. The 1976 and 1985 surveys are ICPSR studies 9211 and 7733, respectively.

DIVORCE THE FINAL ACT IN RELATIONSHIPS

Realize that divorce can be the final act in your marriage. Millions of people end up going through divorce and sadly many of them, never recover. Sure, they may be alive but they are former shells of what they once were.

You can eventually benefit and grow strong but only if you have the strength and family and friends to rally around you. Sometimes this process can take years.

Divorce can rob us of our dignity, wealth and security. Even though it is necessary sometimes, there is always a price for it. Pay attention to what is just, fair and things what will benefit you. It's not ok to allow the soon to be ex to tell you that "I'm taking this and I will leave you that if the split is 70 /30 in favor of them or vice versa."

Divorce is a terrible thing. It fills you with anger, resentment and deep pain. You want the other party to suffer for the betrayal. You actually begin to plot another human being's suffering. Didn't you used to love him or her? So how can you dislike them so much that you want them to suffer?

You need to learn how to let go of the pain right way. Anything else can prevent you from growing happy and healthy. Your life can degenerate into a "fatal Attraction" scenario that can end up costing you deep and lasting pain. Divorce is NOT fashionable even though statistics tells us otehrwise.

We want to encourage YOU to move into a happier place. Will it be easy? NO! Can you conquer your fears and misgivings? Of course, but then some of you might also need someone to help you through this. Like a wounded man on the battlefield, your chances of survival double if there is a friend to help carry you off the field.

Life will always have its challenges and that old theory "no pain no gain" comes to mind here. However, this is what helps us to build character, learn from our choices and grow to be healthier and stronger. Your reactions to these challenges either teach you or make you withdraw in pain. What will your choice be?

Knowing the truth sets you free, acting upon it, is necessary for those around you to realize that you will no longer be the dirt beneath someone else's feet, or the person who is afraid to speak up in the right way, not just react to it.

Grow strong, be happy and choose a path that will benefit others not just you. You know you can achieve this, by proving to yourself that you are worthy and will no longer think otherwise.

NEVER DOUBT THAT ANYONE CAN BECOME
A WARRIOR

There exist in our society people that will never play fair. I put this book together because quite frankly, some people are monsters and you need this information to protect yourself and your family from them.

Your ex might not have been capable of unspeakable acts in the past but statistics show that during divorce this can quickly change.

Will your ex move on with his - her life or will he become one of those people who can never let it go? Will they become a true monster . . . filled with rage and anger seeking to hurt you?

Sometimes this means the worst possible outcome. Here is where you must get involved to protect yourself, your home, your life and stand guard ready to defend yourself. It is an attitude of power.

But how? How does any person truly protect themselves?

This book is now your great equalizer. Learn from those who have gone down this dark road and lived to tell the tale.

The information here can literally save your life and finances. It will become your body armor and if need be – a weapon of powerful defense.

There are monsters are out there. Could your Ex become one or maybe he or she already is? No matter how hard you try to be civil sometimes, in the end, their rage and anger could end up endangering your life.

Some people are truly capable of becoming psychopaths and only need right stimulus or trigger. Divorce can be the straw that broke the camel's back and cause the Ex to become a REAL threat.

"The truth of this matter is that we are all monsters just beneath our social masks waiting for the right moment to consume and destroy." – Unknown Author

We decided to explore this darker area of people's behavior, because it is important to understand how everyone is capable of becoming a Dr Jekyll and Mr. Hyde.

We asked men who were divorcing what their **darkest fantasy was and if they could get away with it what they might do to their former wife.** What we discovered was horrifying.

Brace yourself; these are actual statements of men involved in divorce: "I'd like to slowly strangle the bitch and watch the color run from her face!"

"Rape her, cut her throat and leave her in the woods . . ."

"I want to tie up the %$# and hang her from a tree to die in slow agony."

"Yeah tell that @ucking whore I'm gonna kill her some day . . ."

"She will never get away from me. Someday I'm sure she will die (by my hand)."

These statements varied in intensity –and there were more some very graphic. Sorry to say that these statements were from some cases where actual interviews took place.

Surprisingly enough some of those above quotes were from men who were higher educated and in a seething rage about getting divorce too. Men view divorce as a gladiatorial confrontation – a winner take all. It is hardwired in their behavior sometimes. They believe that it is all or nothing.

The majority of men who were interviewed all wanted to get even with their ex and a majority were working on ways to make the woman pay dearly in some form or another. Even it wasn't physical violence it certainly would be through other means.

That is the truth of it! Almost ALL of these men were plotting to deeply HURT their former spouse. This reason alone you need to understand. You have to be ready.

We will discuss later on non threatening ways you can try to get his anger dissipated so that he does NOT grow truly horrible to you. Still these do not always work.

We bring this up because this is how seriously we want you to take this revelation. We have discovered that most people underestimate even what they consider intellectually inferior during a divorce. This is something you must never do.

We are assuming that you have exhausted every way to have a civil divorce here. I think you need to at some point approach your ex and beg him to keep this whole affair civil, especially if you have children.

You MUST find a way to allow your Ex to vent their rage in a non-destructive manner and allow them to vent their frustrations or this can happen. We will discuss this later how to even allow him to yell at you to prevent this from happening.

Despite the fact that advocacy groups like NOW have worked for two decades to halt the epidemic of gender-based violence and sexual assault, the numbers are still shocking.

For example, In 2005, 1,181 women were murdered by an intimate partner. That's an average of three women every day. Of all the women murdered in the U.S., about one-third was killed by an intimate partner.

These predatory people do not warrant the title of "human". Our prisons are filled with people who killed, sometimes horrifically, their ex.

Had any of these women had a plan (studies show that most did not) they may have survived. No one likes to believe someone you were married to could ever do this. Yet every year over 1,000 women are often brutally slain by former intimate partners.

Sorry, but you HAVE TO listen to this, especially if you know EXACTLY what I am saying about your spouse or partner.

Many of the tactics in this book discusses ways to "Detect & Protect and even create a pressure valve" so at least you have a chance to diffuse these walking time bombs and they can work.

No plan is foolproof but if you follow these tactics the advantage is yours. These tactics are grouped in basic levels of protection that anyone can do. We spent a great deal of time interviewing security experts to provide this information. Of course if your situation is truly bad you might need to hire a professional to protect you.

We will also discuss tactics that work to get harassment to stop. Perhaps your ex would never want to hurt you physically but is trying to make you pay in other ways. We cover all of this as well in the next pages.

PROTECTION WORKS IN SEVERAL WAYS

Security Basics:

Barriers – is your first line of defense between you and your adversary. There are several ways you can create barriers.

Some barriers are psychological in nature and physical as well. For example your first step is creating barriers is that you might construct a fence around your property.

Or set electronic motion detectors on your property. Certainly an alarm system is a great start with large signs out front saying THIS PROPERTY Protected by ABC Alarm System (psychological barrier as well) and now costs as little as 100 bucks down and 20 bucks a month.

If you can't afford an alarm system consider this: you might end up dead if you do not. Alarm systems do more than just make noise.

Modern monitoring services can detect intruders, detect open doors, open windows, fire, carbon monoxide, even water and smoke damage. They can instantly alert the police, call you if you are away from your home or protected area the instant an intruder breaks in (possibly saving your life) contact fire department and ambulance even if you can't.

The panic button features or motion detection that is set after you go to bed will allow you to sleep relatively peacefully. Cheap and effective you should first implement this because security systems work well **to frighten off intruders** as well and will discourage theft or vandalism of your property.

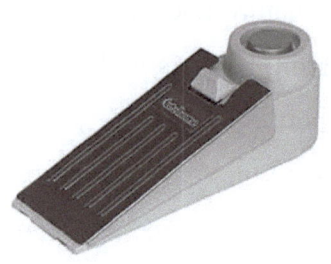 Of course if you live in an apartment, you can do a few things to protect yourself. Doorjamb alarms emit 125 DB of ear splitting sound if it is moved touched, stepped on or a door is opened even a little on it.

Cheap insurance and the noise generated will tell your assailant that you know they are trying to break in your premises. Similar alarms exist for windows and these alarms are all under 20 dollars.

Many are under fifteen dollars and can be wired to a main alarm set up to trigger and call you, the police and even give an audible warning that an intruder can hear, "Warning you have been detected and the police have been called!" –"I know you are breaking in my home – the police have been called and I'm upstairs with a loaded shotgun and will kill you if you do not leave!"

In studies even determined thieves, burglars even those bent on doing you harm hearing this often retreated – to be apprehended later by a method I will also share with you later.

 Apartment living can also include personal alarm systems like the one shown here by mace – the wireless Security System consists of a main control unit with a 105 dB alarm, one door/window sensor, one motion detector sensor and a remote control with panic button.

The system can accommodate up to 14 additional wireless and/or direct wired sensors (window, motion detectors, pressure pads) so you can place protection all over an apartment without defacing anything.

You can even program your cell phone and additional emergency contact phone numbers into the control unit. If the alarm is triggered while you're away, the control unit will dial the first number of the programmed list. The person answering the call will hear a pre-recorded message and have the option to listen in on the room, broadcast their voice through the control unit, or disarm the system.

Please understand we are not trying to sell you security products here. We just wanted you to have an idea of what exists that creating barriers is affordable and capable of protecting your property and allow you to sleep at night.

An entire variety of products exist that can fit your lifestyle as well as offer you protection like Mace, pepper spray and other forms of personal protection . Carrying a spray around on you in the event of an attack can give you enough time to escape your attacker or EX spouse.

Ok so we have covered protection of your property. This should include at some point a way for you to be able to know who is OUTSIDE your premises and around your home. If you live in a home let me again suggest you consult with a security agent like Life Shield or ADT home security or a similar company.

TOP TEN SECURITY TIPS
IN CREATING "BARRIERS"

Purchasing homeowners insurance or renter's insurance is a good idea for a couple of reasons. You should always keep your **documents** (like divorce papers, passports, birth certificates and restraining orders), your valuables with a video recorder and place this recording in a safety deposit box away from the premises.

Why Insurance?

Imagine a fire, theft or burglary. If your ex decides you have something he or she wants or doesn't want you to have, a vengeful house fire could happen. It is also smart to protect yourself and such insurance like renters is effective. Store your most expensive items, documents in a safety deposit box or fake storage container (hollowed out book, fake in plain site safe)

Research wireless and motion infra red cameras (very affordable kits exist for a few hundred dollars or less) that can record, broadcast and be moved easily to any location and even be disguised to look like other items.

Make sure every camera you purchase or safety system can produce date and time stamps. It will be a lifesaver in a court room if need be.

 For more info check out:

http://www.4hiddenspycameras.com/

Lock doors and windows every time you leave the house and when you are HOME as well. I know it sounds simple but most people do NOT lock their doors during the day when they are home. You must lock your doors at all times (barrier principle).

Join neighborhood watch or start one – One of the most overlooked strategies for self protection and it costs nothing. Yet even a watchful neighbor (especially older people would love something to do like this) can prevent a crime. Extra eyes are critical – and even if you don't find many people to be part of this kind of organization you can post flyers all over where you live saying this community is a neighborhood watch community.

Make sure you post these flyers everywhere where you live and surrounding your neighborhood form every way your ex might travel to get to your home. This kind of psychological alerting to would be thieves (and angry Ex's) could deter them from committing crimes against you.

What if you simply can't afford an alarm system?

Here is cheap deterrence for a few dollars – **Amazon sell these stickers**

Place these security stickers on the windows of your home or car to announce to would-be intruders that your property is protected by an alarm system.

These stickers are a great deterrent whether or not they are actually used with an alarm. Thieves are looking for the easiest home or car to burglarize. The presence of these stickers can cause them to pass by your property in search of an easier target.

Portable Concealed Self Protection

Non-lethal protection is your best bet. Why? Most states legally allow you to carry things like mace, pepper spray, stun guns and similar protection devices.

The absolute best protection device is something like a ring or watch – and you keep it on your person all the times even when you sleep; always ready to defend yourself. A direct spray into an assailant's face will more than likely allow you to get away.

What About Firearms?

Guns are an absolute weapon of final choice. I do believe there is a place for a firearm in your home (read below) Please understand that weapons of this magnitude require training, safe handling and absolute control for using it – as well as knowledge of the law so that your self defense does not end up as YOU going to prison for a very long time.

Use of mace, stun guns or non lethal defense shows you had no intent of killing someone – and important consideration if you ever end up in court. Discharging a firearm could end with an innocent person dead and you having to live with hanging over your head, for the rest of your life.

A Better Tactic -

Flee To a Safe room or safe location –even if you live in an apartment you can set up a place (like in the back of your closet) where if any of your alarms go off – you immediately flee to. In this location are implements of self – defense and a communication device.

Let's face facts, even though you may have a restraining order on your Ex what are the chances that the police will be at your residence in time, if they decide to break into your home?

In some cases the police are so overwhelmed now that unless there is a murder involved you are NOT on the top of their list. So you have to make plans for the JUST IN CASE scenario's.

LEARN THE SKILLFUL ART OF NEGOTIATION

Learning to be clever in the negotiation practices in the middle of a divorce can be a huge tipping point in your favor. While the Ex spouse may become angry or emotional across the table in front of lawyers, you have to learn to become almost stoic in your behavior and thinking.

The information contained here is for information purposes only.

There is a speaker in the USA called Roger Dawson. He is one of the best when it comes to negotiating deals. Roger holds seminars where he teaches people how to become better at this art too. Success magazine called him "America's Premier Business Negotiator."

When you go through divorce it defiantly becomes like a business negotiation, so there is a point as to why we are using Roger as an example of becoming incredibly smart at negotiation.

Too many times we involve our personal feelings and emotions into our divorces and while that is completely understandable it may NOT be in your best interest. If you can look at this whole divorce situation like a business deal gone badly, you would be much better off. Take the emotion out of the picture for time being and just get what is owed to you!

Rules To The Games Of Divorce Warfare

Rule: Plan what you are going to do FIRST and Foremost.

I can't stress this enough. Too many people just leave with no outlets or systems set in place to help them when in the middle of a divorce.

Sometimes you have no recourse but to LEAVE in abusive situations, and that is completely understandable. The safest thing for you is to be gone if the abuse is becoming more than you can bare.

Make sure the new environment you move to is less stressful so that you can start to plan for the success of your part in the divorce. Start with a check list of what you want to achieve, your new living arrangements, the finances and anything else that needs to be discussed and shared. Stick with the list; do not be persuaded to lower your list standards by your spouse or deviate from your goal.

Rule: Just because you don't have any money doesn't mean you cannot get a divorce.

Legal Aid has some restrictions on it you will need to check them out. Emotional abuse is not really something they will help you with.

However if you are being physically abused, you may be able to get help from them. Much of this kind of help is based on your income and the severity of the case in question.

Women's Shelters are excellent sources of Information too. Get a temporary custody order of your children first if you believe yourself to be the better parent. This will give you more bargaining power in the court room if you have put this procedure in place right from the start. Get a restraining order too. If you are being harassed and physically hurt there is a record of the court documents. These are easy to get.

You will also need the last Years Taxation paperwork that was lodged with the IRS dept. Most legal documents want to see your and the husbands income. Keep pay stubs if you have them as well.

Social Security cards and all other forms of Identification keep this handy at all times. You can and are very capable of doing your own divorce if your funds are very limited.

Rule: Your financial status should be changed out ASAP

You need money, bank account access and other very important things. Get a personal savings or checking account with only YOUR name on it **BEFORE**, you leave your husband. If you are getting direct deposit into your joint checking account change it to your PERSONAL checking account ASAP.

As long as you have a joint checking account your spouse can take every last penny out of the account and there is nothing legally you can do about it. Play it safe and have your accounts set up quickly to protect your own interests.

Assets like your home, land, property, cars and IRA's will need to be completed on your financial paperwork to the court when dividing legally.

You will need to take all of this information to the court house with you when filing for the divorce paperwork. Make at least three copies of everything, this will save you time, energy and frustration when going to the courthouse.

Rule: Keep a daily diary and write everything down in it.

Phone calls to the partner / spouse, dates, times, things said to each other and threats made. This can be a real lifesaver. Understand this, the more evidence you have the more POWER you can use. Don't get mad, get even, the sneaky way.

Diaries are often used in court hearings as evidence. If you are constantly arguing then write down everything that is said. Words said can be used to come back in a court room with a dairy that is filled with notes. The Judge may ask to see your dairy when you are in court.

Believe me a written book of times, dates, places looks really good to a judge.

Rule: Find out where the local county courthouse is.

Get as much information as you can to the online websites there. There is a wealth of resources, support groups, legal advice, paperwork and government agencies that may be able to help you. Each county and state have paperwork you can download and fill out on your own. There are assistants and volunteers that offer you their time and services in filing legal papers correctly. Make an appointment with them. Your local courthouse should be able to put you in touch with these people. I got help this way.

Rule: Make a list of all your Spouse's or Partners Bad Habits. Write down things like; Gambling, Smoking, Drugs, Liquor, On-line Dating. Maybe strip clubs and porn sites, can eat up the biggest paycheck. Keep your ears and eyes open.

Friends, relatives, and even your children may spill the goodies about your spouse. You have to be alert, careful and above all stay calm. Don't sink to the level of the dirty mess you are searching for. DO NOT harass and pester the kids about daddy or mommy. Do not pick your family friends brains either. If your kids accidently mention something worthwhile, write it in the dairy.

If a family friend volunteers information, write it down. Try and stay dignified at all times and never try to deceive other people. This annoys your friends and they may end up speaking against you.

Rule: Never jump at the first offer made to you.

Remember the art of negotiation! NEVER give in too soon or this will give the other party power from the get go. Being able to hold out for more also shows that you are not a push over and you will no longer tolerate anyone being able to dictate what they think you are entitled too. If the soon to be Ex becomes annoyed because you have refused to give into their whims, then this behavior is on them. You just walk away and smile.

Rule: Ask for more than you actually expect to get.

This will give you room to negotiate in the long run. Your first offer should actually be fairly unreasonable. As a matter of fact it should be laughable. This kind of offer will make the other party re-think their strategy too.

Have a final goal in mind of where you want to be and write it down. Get it into your head that you will ONLY negotiate up to that point. You will not go below the acceptance point. Place this goal in a place where you can see it like the refrigerator or a mirror as the psychological battle is already fought in your head.

Rule: Avoid Confrontation in your negotiating

There is nothing worse than seeing two people screaming at each other in a public place. It is demeaning and very childish. It is not good in building character either. Especially if you are trying to impress the Judge and show him or her that you are the bigger person.

Let the spouse or partner throw their temper tantrums while you just walk away in silence from them. Actually silence is a great teacher of people's behavior. When they act like a child, don't treat them like a child, just walk away, completely silent. Just keep going and don't you dare turn around or the other party wins again.

Rule: Use all your power and means available to you.

If you give someone an inch they will usually take a mile. Understand you are in this divorce because you are tired of the same old situation. You are here to win...period!

If you allow the other party to gain control the first time, you may as well give it up, right there. The more you learn about the legal system, negotiations, resources available to you and even a little psychology will save you headaches, time and sanity.

Rule: Do not buy into the emotional and verbal blackmail control babble.

This kind of verbal diarrhea is why you are sitting in the court room to begin with. I thought you were sick of it? The new woman or man is empowered so act like it. Stop giving your power, time and energy to this kind of abuse.

Children are always used as emotional pawns in these types of games. As long as you do not say one unkind word in front of your children about their father or partner, then your kids will figure things out on their own.

Understand your kids are much smarter than your spouse wants YOU to think they are. Tell the Ex that you do not want to discuss the children with him or her unless it is important.

The Ex will nearly always try and use the kids as an emotional crutch to you, if you let them. You are supposed to be the bigger person. The soon to be Ex knows what buttons to push to raise your temper too.

STAY CALM. Change the subject quickly and ask "Is there is anything else?" before you leave or hang up. They will figure out really quickly that you are not buying it anymore.

Question: If one parent is constantly running the other parent down to the children, who do you think your kids will run too?

Answer: The opposite parent who is not running their mouth all the time, that's who.

Rule: Stay Calm, Poised and Very Together At All Times.

This cannot be stressed enough especially when a situation can easily become volatile with face to face contact with the Ex. If you understand there are triggers to set you or the Ex off, then back off and become silent and remove yourself from the situation. Conversations over the telephone need to be calm and almost relaxed, to avoid shouting matches and constant aggravation.

Do not allow the new girlfriend / boyfriend to control YOUR life. You are not here to have your feathers ruffled by the new love. This person is not your mother or father. Their opinions about you or the divorce have no relevance in your life. It is NOT any of their business what is happening in the divorce.

SHE or HE is not your children's parent and their opinion about your parenting skills is just another way to rile you up. Laugh at her / him and tell her to mind her own business in a GROWN UP manner, then become SILENT. Your Ex is counting on agitating YOU but if you remain calm, it throws a huge monkey wrench into the plans.

Calm stoic like behavior, drives people who want to rile others up, into a state of confusion and in the long run it gives you the upper hand.

Did you ever consider that the Ex might actually be counting on you getting upset with the new love? Actually it may have been a planned attack to see how far you will go.

Some Ex spouses especially some male's relish the idea of having two women fighting over them; don't fall for the games and manipulation.

What is the old saying "What goes around comes around?" Remember that it will serve you well.

TOP REASONS WHY PEOPLE FILE FOR DIVORCE

Two of the biggest problems most people face in today's society related to divorce, is a lack of commitment towards their marriage and infidelity.

Commitment may be lacking in one of the partners because the marriage "happened" and they were not really in love. Maybe the wife was pregnant and the husband just did the RIGHT THING to keep the peace within the families. This partner may have felt forced in the marriage and now they are trapped, angry, resentful and bored.

Spouses who are unhappy will NOT be loyal to their partners.

No communication between spouses

Without communication no relationship can work. Keeping your resentments simmering within you is very unhealthy. Your partner does not know what is happening with you, so this is likely to create distance between both of you. An explosive boiling point is the usual result of no communication as one partner eventually looses it on the other.

Abandonment, Alcohol Addiction, Substance Abuse

When one of the partners deserts his or her spouse for a certain time or an indefinite period divorce emerges as the answer. This can even be in the form of spending excessive amounts of time at the local bar. Sitting in the house getting drunk or under the influence of drugs will ultimately cause the relationship to fail too. If one person is doing the drugs and the other is not, there is really not that much the relationship has going for it. The two people are obviously at different ends of the spectrum.

Physical Abuse, Sexual Abuse and Emotional Abuse

These types of abuses are not uncommon and tolerating them is NEVER acceptable. A spouse who loves himself or herself would not put with such abuses on his family or loved one.

Many times we see the other person protect their abusive spouse and even make excuses for the bruises or marks on their bodies. The fact is once you realize the extent of the control in your relationship; the decision can only be one of two choices. Stay and take the abuse or leave and live your life free of abuse.

Inability to manage or resolve conflict

Lack of maturity disables people to manage conflicts and handle personality differences. Young people/teenagers getting married have less of a chance because they do not have enough life experiences to base their lives on. Sometimes this is because of a pregnancy and the two teenagers feel it is better for their child to be married. Usually within a few years they are divorced because of the strain of raising children as no more than children themselves.

Differences in Personal and Career Goals

People who live together before marriage have higher rates of divorce than people who didn't.

Distance enters the marriage and the relationship broadens to the point of complete breakdown. Sometimes the conflict is about jealousy as one spouse is bent on competing with the other over a job or career.

Different expectations about household tasks and financial problems Financial problems can be a major source for problems in a marriage. One partner may feel they carry more of the load and take their frustrations out on the wife or husband. In these cases love can become sour quickly. Feelings of frustration and an inability to change the situation becomes more dominant in the partner taking the load.

Intellectual Inflexibility

Intellectual incompatibility creates misunderstandings. The smarter person feels frustrated, while the less intelligent partner is mad about not reaching the same level, as the other one. The pair makes each other miserable with snide remarks, comments that maybe someone is a grunt at their job while the other is an executive.

Mental Instability or Mental Illness

Sometimes when the spouse becomes deeply depressed the partner may not understand this. It is too frustrating and aggravating for the other person to accept. Also mental illness does not allow space for normal communication between spouses.

Many times after a child is born the wife may go through a depression that seems to take forever to get over and the husband becomes frustrated with her lack of desire to be intimate and say things to her like "You never used to be like this." The wife may be tired, overwhelmed and depressed with the new baby. Lack of understanding and comforting can cause a huge rift in the marriage.

Religious beliefs, cultural and lifestyle differences

Cultural views will eventually clash unless we learn to adapt. Western and Eastern cultures can make a relationship difficult to meld.

The new religion was not what you were married into. The partner may not accept this new religion or even try to understand it. They are feeling left out, angry and betrayed.

When people have valid reasons to divorce, he or she knows it is time. After all, there is no point in hanging on to a person if you can no longer live together.

It is time to move on. . .

THE POWER OVER DIVORCE SITUATIONS AND PEOPLE

Here are eight factors that give YOU **Power over People** and your Situation:

Legitimate and Legal -

Get to know the legal system in your state and county like the back of your hand. Custody situations need to be always handled with care.

Get to know your state legal system intimately. Know the visitation rights of the other parent.

1. If you are looking for total custody then you have to have a good reason. Abuse and neglect could be the reason, and then YOU will need proof to back this up.

2. Take pictures of your kids before they go off to visit their father or other partner.

3. When they come back to you, look at them and their bodies. If there are bruises on their body take more pictures that day.

4. Do NOT pick up the phone and start screaming at your husband or partner about the marks on your child's body.

5. Instead, record and tape all conversations with your spouse over these marks in a controlled and civil manner. It will go better for you in the court room.

6. NEVER question your own children without a witness present, find a neighbor if you have to. You can use this as a testimony in court and it also shows other people how much of a better parent you are.

7. A Judge may order your children have a session with a court appointed Psychologist. You do NOT want to implant your own thoughts into your child's head. This will GO AGAINST you. Your child will speak if you have been loving and honest with them.

8. Explain to your child, that there is nothing to be afraid of. You will always be here to protect them. Just tell the truth, is all you can ask them to do.

Coercive and Persuasive -

By knowing the legal system you will be able to persuade not only the Judge but possibly your spouse as to your power and rights as well.

Especially in the custody cases as I have mentioned above.

The court will decide based on the child's interview what is best in their opinion. If you have taken all the above steps we suggest, I assure you that the Custody situation should not be a problem. Remember the Judge wants a record of everything. The more evidence the better you are off.

Reverent (Worshipped) or Admired -

Even though your spouse may despise you for continually outsmarting him or her in the divorce, let me tell you something, eventually they will respect you.

Never again will they try and pull numerous lies or manipulation on you. YOU are now too SMART for any of that old garbage. Other people and people and family members who never thought; "You had it in you either," will now admire your strength and character in taking charge of your life on your own.

Charisma and Personality -

Do NOT go into the court room looking and feeling like a mouse.

Do you really think you have gained power over your spouse or anyone, looking this way?

What will the Judge think of you?

I can tell you now; people who walk into a court room with their head held high and dressing like a professional…get the judges attention. In their view, you make a good mother - father, a responsible adult and a take charge person.

Your spouse is going to look at you as well.

Do you know what they are going to think? "Wow, he or she has changed." "They look great!"

Inside of themselves, they are going to be churning because you have now just gained the upper hand. You never looked this good before and he or she will not be able to believe the change in you.

This is the message you are trying to get across to everyone; YOU want the soon to be EX, to know that you are better off without him or her. You are doing very well on your own and you are HAPPY.

A business dress code can be everything to win your case.

You are going into court to WIN. Dress and act like a winner! Be forceful but respectful.

Thank the Judge and offer your paperwork at the appropriate time. NEVER interrupt the judge, or your opponent. Just smile and wait your turn. Believe me when your turn comes around, you will have the Judges attention. Present your case in the courtroom, like you were the CEO of a corporation.

Situation and Circumstances -

Breathe the fresh air…YOU can always change your current situation with drive and determination. The best thing of all is that you can become wealthy or financially secure and your Ex-spouse or Partner cannot claim a penny if you make them sign this off in court first!

Ha...how do you like me now Ex?

Your –In- Laws may not believe all of your problems with their son – daughter at first, but eventually at some point he or she will slip up and they will see with their own eyes. Once again remain silent and it will speak for itself in time.

Expertise and Knowledge -

You have to become a bookworm sometimes in order to get what information you need. Gather as much information as you can on the internet, library and other resources. Join an online notice board for other divorced women - men. Most of these people have been through the same ordeals and they can help. I'm serious here! Some of these people have incredible ideas.

Most lawyers will offer you a free consultation on your first visit. The phone book is full of them. Look a few up in your neighborhood and pay them all a call. Get free legal advice until you are sure you know what you are doing. Then go down to the courthouse and start filing.

The Fees in each state differ but it's usually not too much. Check whether or not the court decides that you and your spouse need to an intermediary, for the sake of the children or not too. That might cost you a little more.

Information and Wisdom.

The smarter you get the less likely your Ex will ever be able to take advantage of you again, especially in the courtroom where it will really counts the most.

The soon to be Ex Partner or Spouse may become unbelievably cruel at times. As long as you know ahead of the game what to expect then you can at least go into the divorce fighting a fair fight. Knowledge is power. You had better believe it!

Your Ex may be throwing you all this flowery stuff at you about trying to remain good friends for the sake of the children. When in actual fact they may be secretly getting taking you for a ride.

These are some of the more common manipulations:

Taking all the money out your joint checking and savings accounts. Get yourself a separate account before you leave him!!

Making plans behind your back to out maneuver you in court.

He or she maybe taking notes on you too.

Psychologically, mentally, emotionally trying to break you down.

Crying on your shoulder, that he still loves you to keep you off his back.

Sometimes the spouse will try and make YOU out to be the bad parent.

If you have to go to mediation over the children do not allow him or her to pick the psychologist for the kids. Let the kids pick. He or she may even try and call the doctor first. They will try to make themselves out to be a martyr and smelling like roses before you even get to speak to the doctor yourself.

Reward and Final Goal.

Figure out really quickly what it is you want the end result to be from your Divorce. Some women and men see it as the end of the world.

I have heard "but I still love him or her and maybe we can still make it work." That's usually going backwards and not looking forward. Just remember why you are here at this point to begin with. You are more than likely missing what is comfortable to you. That is all.

Remember we do become vulnerable all over again, if you allow it into your life. The first thing a lot of women or men go out and do is find a new love. This is a very BAD MISTAKE!

Find out who you are first.

Someone else may have always told you who were, but that is not really true. A new relationship should only happen when you are completely healed and whole. Then you have a better chance of meeting someone more genuine and compatible.

Spend some time with yourself everyday. Thirty minutes is a life saver, so shut the world and family out in that time. Light some candles around the bathtub and SINK into it. Don't wallow in self pity and woe is me for months after you are officially divorced.

YOU need to begin your life again. This time do it the right way.

Go back to school if you want to. Take a class in fun stuff if that's what you want. Start a community group of single women –men and children and make new friends. There are plenty of coffee houses you can all meet at. Picnics can be fun this way too. Get out there and LIVE YOUR LIFE!

How to Verbally Destroy your Opponent in Court

Under the **Rules Section** you are keeping your diary…right?

You were also keeping a written log of all your spouses' bad habits?

You have gathered some credible and exposing information about your spouse. Use all of these bad behaviors into your motions in court.

Expose everything in a way that shows the necessary connections.

If it's for custody you want to show yourself as the most responsible and caring parent.

For child support issues, you want to prove to the court why your husband can afford to pay your children more than he currently is. Stay Calm and Composed as you present to the Judge.

Do not go overboard:

If he or she is paying support and you are primarily fighting about assets, do not tell the judge he or she goes to strip joints or nightclubs. There is no reason to intentionally hurt your own financial status, by totally enraging your spouse.

You need only prove the points necessary to your case. If he or she is not paying his support then the judge needs to know what they are doing with their money. Let the judge know then, what the money is being spent on.

If they are getting more than his or her fair share of assets the judge needs a very clear and precise breakdown of what assets you each have, and who has what claims, the children, etc.

Always remember that what you put out in public can always come back at you. Court houses keep tons of records and some of these are accessible in the public arena too.

Do not involve your children in the battle. They do not need to see a smear campaign involving their parents. They love you both and it's not fair to put them in the middle.

CONCLUSION

We hope this book has enabled you to understand more about the dynamics of divorce and how to achieve your goals with a better outcome.

Of course each one of us can always choose to be a victim or come out on the other end as a healthier, happier person.

Sometimes guerilla warfare tactics are in order with divorce. It seems in some cases we are left with no other alternative. Whatever decisions you choose to make in the divorce will be because of a good basis of knowledge and understanding.

Our hope is that this book was able to equip you with the insights you need to start off on the right foot and stay ahead of the game.

We wish you all the best in your future as a happier and free individual.

Printed by Libri Plureos GmbH in Hamburg,
Germany